Hawks for Kids

by Sumner Matteson
photography by John Hendrickson
illustrated by John F. McGee

NORTHWORD
PRESS, INC
Minocqua, Wisconsin

DEDICATION

To Indra, Beatrice, Deneb, and Liila.
May you always have a chance
to see a hawk in a bright fall sky!

Designed by Kenneth Hey

For a free catalog describing NorthWord's line of nature books and gift items, call 1-800-336-5666.

Library of Congress Cataloging-in-Publication Data
Matteson, Sumner.
    Hawks for kids / by Sumner W. Matteson.
      p. cm.
    ISBN 1-55971-462-X
      1. Hawks—Juvenile literature. [1. Hawks.] I. Title.
  QL696. F32M27 1995   94-40922
  598.9'16—dc20   CIP
                    AC

Printed in Hong Kong

One early spring day two girls were quietly hiking when something big and gray caught their attention on the ground ahead. Allison saw it first. "What's that?" she exclaimed, pointing. Her sister Amanda turned to look. Underneath a spruce tree, a crow-sized, blue-gray hawk stood over a dead cottontail rabbit.

"It's the Cooper's Hawk! He's back from last year," whispered Allison.

"What's he doing?" asked Amanda.

Clenching its sharp talons to tightly grip the rabbit's body, the Cooper's Hawk used its hooked bill to tear off and eat chunks of meat. Then it flew off into the woods.

The Cooper's Hawk had returned from its winter home. Cooper's Hawks migrate each year in the spring and fall and some spend the winter as far south as Costa Rica.

"Let's call Prakash," said Allison. "He'll want to know about this."

Prakash is a tall, thin man with a gray beard, and he lives in the forest and studies hawks. All the kids call him "Hawk Man" because of his knowledge of hawks. He even looks like a hawk. His nose is big like a hawk's cere, the waxlike upper part of the hawk's bill. But unlike hawks, he wears glasses. And he smiles a lot.

He once told the girls about hawks having two tiny pits in each eye, called fovea, located at the back of the eye, that allow them to see great distances very clearly. He said, "We humans only have one of these pits in each eye. A tree-perched Cooper's Hawk would have no problem seeing me far away. So in most cases hawks probably see you before you see them, unless they're recently hatched young, which are born blind."

When the girls got home from their hike, Allison left a message for Prakash about the return of the Cooper's Hawk. The next evening Prakash arrived eager to hear about the bird they saw.

Cooper's Hawk

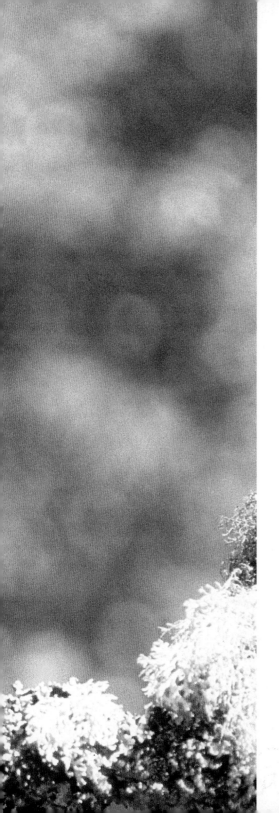

"I was worried about the hawks in the storm last night," sighed Allison. "I found the nest and was afraid it was going to blow out of the tree. But it probably won't fall off because it's held up by the V of the tree limbs, and even another branch coming up from the side. Come on. We'll show you."

After a bit of a walk, they found the nest again. "Look! Up there! There it is!" pointed Allison to a slender, high oak tree. The stick nest was about 40 feet above the ground and clearly visible in a stand of trees that had not yet begun to leaf out. The "cak–cak–cak" call of the Cooper's Hawk rang out from the woods.

Cooper's Hawk

Cooper's Hawks often come into a woods to scout out where they've nested the previous year, and sometimes they use the last year's nest. But usually they build a new nest in the area, often on top of an old squirrel nest or hawk nest.

The male does most of the nest building, bringing in sticks and twigs to a site that may be 20 to 60 feet high. The nest is built to be partially shaded by the tree tops once all the leaves open.

Northern Goshawk

The male is a really energetic fellow, sometimes building two or three nests!

The female lays 3 to 5 bluish-white eggs in the nest. The eggs become kind of dirty white as incubation goes on.

When the female incubates her eggs she sits so tightly on them that it's difficult to see her from below. This is true of all hawks. She spends most of the time on the eggs while the male is perched nearby or out catching prey.

Usually the only time she'll leave the nest during the incubation period is when he calls and lets her know he's got a meal for her, which he does about three times a day.

Then he flies up to the nest and incubates the eggs while she is perched on a limb eating her meal. After 30 to 36 days, the eggs hatch.

Amanda asked, "Will they hatch when school is through? What will they look like?"

Prakash said, "Cooper's Hawk young begin to hatch out in early to mid June so you'll be out of school. When they hatch, they, and for that matter all hawk nestlings, are covered with a light coat of white down and are quite weak, only able to stretch their heads to take food.

Cooper's Hawks

"Soon, a thicker down replaces the original coat, allowing the nestlings to withstand rains and cold temperatures if left alone for a short while by their parents.

"The first feathers grow in on the wings and tail, then the body. By then the young are more than a few weeks old and are moving about the nest, picking at sticks or fresh green leafy sprigs brought into the nest to make home a little more clean.

"When they have to relieve themselves, hawk young will move to the edge of the nest, lift their tails a little, and poop over the nest edge, scattering whitewash on the ground below. It's quite a sight!"

Sharp-shinned Hawk

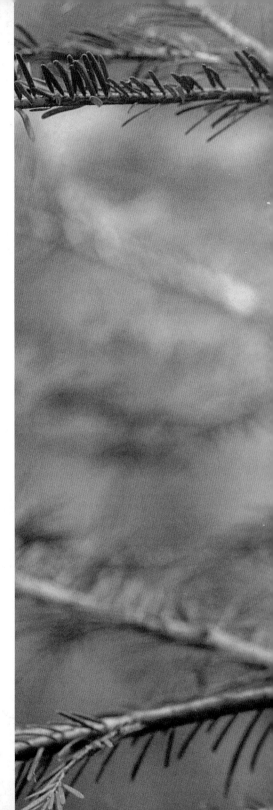

Later that fall, Prakash brought Allison and Amanda to a ridge to watch hawks, where in September and October something very special happens.

On a clear day following the arrival of cool weather, hundreds of hawks pass overhead. Northwesterly winds hit the ridge, which heats up under a bright sun, and warm air climbs upward. Hawks use the updrafts, called thermals, to help them fly south.

Hundreds of hawks migrate from areas in the north to escape the coming winter snows. There is less food available for them to eat in winter; this is why so many must migrate south.

As they watched for signs of the migrating birds, Prakash talked. "Standing on this ridge, you wonder how far they will go today. Hawks don't like to cross open water, but will if they must, and so often they fly for miles above a narrow shore or coastline."

sprey

And just as if on cue, Allison and Amanda saw a group of hawks approaching, and shouted together, "Look! Look at them!"

Red-tailed Hawk

They soared and circled upward, lifted by billowy winds until the thermals started to cool high in the sky and could no longer carry them. Just as that happened, they saw distant hawks riding other thermals, and watched the close birds flap and glide to join them.

As they watched, Prakash told them that hawks that migrate in flocks, such as the Broad-winged Hawk, Sharp-shinned Hawk, and Red-tailed Hawk in the eastern United States, and Swainson's Hawk in the West, are the most numerous during fall migration.

"Imagine hundreds of Broad-winged Hawks at one time migrating south. Together, they form large groups called kettles that fill the sky. When it gets rainy, however, or winds shift strongly to the south, these hawks may perch in trees or rest on the ground, waiting for favorable winds from the northwest again," said Prakash.

Most hawks migrate during the day so people have a great opportunity to see many of them. Four of the most famous places in North America to see hundreds, and sometimes (if you're lucky) thousands, of migrating hawks during a clear, cool fall day are: Cape May on the New Jersey coast off the Atlantic Ocean, Hawk Mountain on the Kittatinny Ridge of eastern Pennsylvania, Hawk Ridge in Duluth, Minnesota, and Point Pelee in Ontario.

"I think the Cooper's Hawk is really special." Prakash asked, "Do you know why?"

Amanda looked at Allison—both shook their heads, no.

"Because it is a member of a special group of birds known as the accipiters. And guess what the word accipiter means? It means 'hawk' in Latin. In fact, of all 39 species of hawks found across North America, the accipiters are considered to be our only true hawks."

"Cool!" said Allison, "And we had a pair nesting right near our house! So, are there other kinds of accipiters?"

"Yeah, and do you like them more than any other hawks in the whole wide world?" smiled Amanda, with a wide grin.

"Well," started Prakash. "There are two other kinds of accipiters in North America. The Sharp-shinned Hawk, the smallest of the three, is among the most numerous hawks in the sky during its September and October migration. The Northern Goshawk is the largest and most powerful of the three and especially fierce when defending its nest. I know of one man who really got clobbered by a Goshawk. He was almost knocked out of a tree when he tried to climb and get near the nest.

Cooper's Hawk

Sharp-shinned Hawk

Northern Goshawk on next page

"Look at the two Sharp-shins over there. You can always tell accipiters by their long tails, short rounded wings, and long legs. When you see them flying in the open sky they typically take five flaps and a short sail. They mainly eat small birds, but from time to time they will also take snakes, lizards, and small to fairly large mammals.

"Accipiters are among my favorite hawks because of the way they skirt through a forest after prey, using shrubs and trees to hide their movements, flashing swiftly by branches and tree trunks, cutting left then right, down then around, over and through the woods, almost as if the trees weren't there!" Prakash used his hands and arms to slice the air like imaginary accipiter wings.

The girls listened closely to his every word, imagining they were flying along with a hawk through the forest.

"Now when the Cooper's Hawk is after its prey, it will move its legs like this." Stepping under a nearby tree, Prakash grabbed an overhead limb to swing his legs forward and up. "Imagine sharp talons on the end of my boots. On making contact, the hawk's wings fan out to break its forward momentum. Both feet grasp the animal, and its talons pierce right through the skin. Hawks are carnivorous; they eat other animals to survive.

"And during the breeding season," continued Prakash, "which runs from April until well into July, the male will capture nearly all the food for the female, although she is bigger than he is."

"How big?" asked Amanda.

"He weighs about 10 to 14 ounces, not quite a pound. She'll weigh over a pound, about 17 to 24 ounces. But she actually looks quite a bit bigger.

"Cooper's Hawk young fledge, or fly, when they are about 30 to 34 days old. Mom and Dad will still bring food to them for a while, and the young will remain near the nest for about 5 or 6 weeks. Then they leave home to explore the area and begin hunting on their own before migration begins."

Osprey on next page

"Prakash, what's the fastest hawk in the world?" asked Amanda loudly.

"I've never seen a Peregrine, but I've heard they're really fast!" remarked Allison.

"Peregrines are indeed fast," started Prakash. "Once, a small plane was flying near a flock of ducks and going about 175 miles per hour. Out of nowhere came a Peregrine Falcon, looking for supper, and passed the plane!"

The Peregrine is a little over a foot tall and has a wingspan over 3 feet. Females are larger than males and weigh up to 2 pounds, compared to about 1-1/2 pounds for the male. They have a dark moustache-like mark that characterizes this grayish-blue bird; the immatures or young are brown.

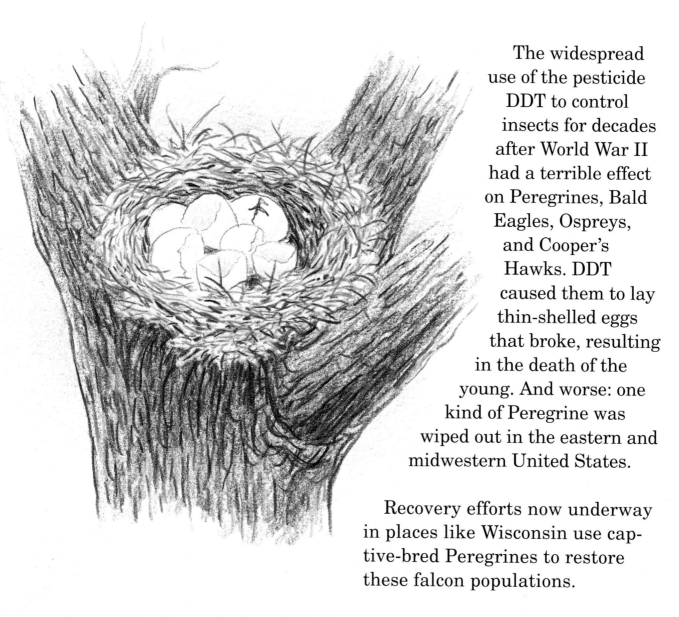

The widespread use of the pesticide DDT to control insects for decades after World War II had a terrible effect on Peregrines, Bald Eagles, Ospreys, and Cooper's Hawks. DDT caused them to lay thin-shelled eggs that broke, resulting in the death of the young. And worse: one kind of Peregrine was wiped out in the eastern and midwestern United States.

Recovery efforts now underway in places like Wisconsin use captive-bred Peregrines to restore these falcon populations.

As evening approached, and the hawks were fewer in the skies, they headed for home. On the way, Allison and Amanda asked when they could watch for other hawks.

Prakash suggested that in August, American Kestrels, another kind of falcon, start frequenting the telephone wires in good numbers in the countryside, and buteo migration starts to get underway.

"What's a buteo?" asked Allison.

He answered, "Buteo in Latin is another word for a kind of hawk. And buteos are another group of birds in the Hawk and Eagle Family. They're more numerous and widespread than the accipiters, and they have long, broad, rounded wings, short broad tails, and short legs and feet."

Red-tailed Hawk

Buteos eat mice, frogs, snakes, lizards, birds, and turtles. Probably the two most well known buteos are the Broad-winged Hawk and the Red-tailed Hawk, with the Broad-wing's counterpart being the Swainson's Hawk out west.

Red-tails, which often occur in the Upper Midwest throughout the year, are the most common hawk. It's a bird seen throughout North America in every state in the nation, wherever open lands and woodlands occur.

This is a hawk that will hunt mice and other rodents, rabbits, squirrels, insects, and even fish. Red-tails like to nest in the tallest tree at the edge of a woods, building a nest 35 to 90 feet above the ground. In areas without trees, they will nest in a shrub or cactus, and even on a craggy cliff.

Red-tailed Hawks

In Wisconsin, Red-tails may begin building a nest or repairing last year's nest as early as late February. A typical bulky nest in southern Wisconsin may be lined with corn husks and cobs.

"How far south do the Broad-wings go?" asked Allison.

"Good question," said Prakash. "Broad-wings are long-distance neotropical migrants, as are Turkey Vultures and Ospreys, flying all the way to Central and South America, thousands of miles away. During fall migration they are far and away the most abundant hawk east of the Mississippi River. Would you believe that 15,000 to 25,000 Broad-wings may be seen on a peak day at Hawk Ridge in September?"

"Incredible!" said Allison, shaking her head slowly.

"Hawks are so cool!" affirmed Amanda, throwing up her hands.

*Red-tailed Hawk on next page
and last page*

"Yes, and I'll just add this about all of them," said Prakash, growing more quiet. "Hawks are important ecologically because they help maintain balanced prey populations. Without them there would be few natural checks on prey population growth.

"Wherever they occur in this land, hawks are spectacular sights that give us a sense of freedom, independence, and even courage."